SERVANT LEADERSHIP

Oluwagbemiga Olowosoyo

©2014 Oluwagbemiga Olowosoyo.

ISBN 978-978-48870-7-6

1 Grand Street,
Bridgeport.
CT 06604
Tel: +12035053614, +12404423634

P. O. Box 36706,
Dugbe, Ibadan
Oyo State, Nigeria
Tel: +234(0)8034652119, +234(0)8056257056

E. Mail: olowosoyo@yahoo.com

Website: www.olowosoyo.org

Bible quotes are from the New King James Version unless otherwise stated.

Dedication

I want to dedicate this book to

Pastor Joseph Takon

who was my leader in college and jolted me out of mediocrity in writing.
I am forever grateful.

Contents

Chapter One

FOLLOW MY EXAMPLE

Jesus, knowing that the Father had given all things into His hands, and that He had come from God and was going to God, rose from supper and laid aside His garments, took a towel and girded Himself. After that, He poured water into a basin and began to wash the disciples' feet, and to wipe them with the towel with which He was girded. Then He came to Simon Peter. And Peter said to Him, "Lord, are You washing my feet?" Jesus answered and said to him, "What I am doing you do not understand now, but you will know after this." Peter said to Him, "You shall never wash my feet!" Jesus answered him, "If I do not wash you, you have no part with Me." Simon Peter said to Him, "Lord, not my feet only,

7

but also my hands and my head!" Jesus said to him, "He who is bathed needs only to wash his feet, but is completely clean; and you are clean, but not all of you." For He knew who would betray Him; therefore He said, "You are not all clean." So when He had washed their feet, taken His garments, and sat down again, He said to them, "Do you know what 1 have done to you? "You call me Teacher and Lord, and you say well, for so 1 am. "If 1 then, your Lord and Teacher, have washed your feet, you also ought to wash one another's feet. "For 1 have given you an example, that you should do as 1 have done to you. "Most assuredly, 1 say to you, a servant is not greater than his master; nor is he who is sent greater than he who sent him."If you know these things, blessed are you if you do them.

John 13:3-17

Unfortunately, the devil has succeeded in diverting the attention of the church from the focus of the Lord in this story by trying to change that event into a miracle event. But the focus was different. Jesus was simply showing us how to be God-approved kind of leaders.

The Middle East is very dusty, that is why the people always cover their heads with shawl, and wear several layers of clothes.

Before you enter into a house, you would need to wash your feet. For that reason water is always provided at the entrance for you. However, when the host is wealthy, he provides slaves to wash your feet for you. No free born would do that for another.

However, in the story above, they were not just entering the house; therefore Jesus was not doing that for necessity, but to communicate something very great to his disciples.

Also, he was not trying to perform miracles here like some Bible teachers insinuate, because only his disciples were with him. And there was no record of any miracle that happened there.

Lessons from the story:

1. In verse 3, the Bible explains the mind-frame of Jesus. He knew who he was in God's sight. He was not measuring himself by the kind of service he rendered.

I remember some years ago, in preparation for a convention; we assigned somebody to take part in washing the toilet, and some individuals went to ask her whether she had offended me to warrant that assignment. They believed that washing the toilet was reserved for the lowest people.

Anyone who measures himself by assignment would always have a complex. Also, I gave an assignment to someone to do some work in a remote place and some of his colleagues hailed him. I was shocked when he reacted sharply.

People like that have no understanding of who they are. They think they become greater when God send them to America, London or any other great city.

They assumed greatness when addressed as Apostle, Prophet, Pastor, Etc; and insulted when called Brother or Sister.

2. In verse 4, He took off his garment, and left only the tunic. Now, at that time, the inner robes of men are always the same, only the outer one depicts your status. When he took off the outer garment, he simply took off his

glory and class. And took on the status of the common man.

Leadership is not always about glory and honour.

Unfortunately this is the opposite of what happens in church today. We believe that since you are a leader you must not mingle with people again. You want to eat secretly.

It is assumed that leaders are not meant to do menial jobs any longer.

I remember when we acquired a land for church some years ago, for financial reasons I requested the church to come and clear the place on Saturday. As I parked my car, and got out with my big cutlass, one of my Assistant Pastors who had come earlier without any cutlass was shocked. He shouted 'abomination' and rushed to meet me at the car to collect the cutlass from me. I simply quoted a scripture to him. 'lest there be enough for us and you, go ye rather to them that sell..'. Eventually he went home to pick his own implement, and joined the good work.

Another time, during one of our major meetings: Eagles Convention. Around 12 midnight, everyone had retired to their rooms, while I was washing the toilets; one of the guests came to ease himself and ran into me. He nearly had a fit. He spent much time disturbing my service, begging me to hand over to him. How can I possibly hand over my own service to anyone?

A brother told me what he experienced some years ago when he rented a house on the same street with his pastor, who was probably younger.

Each time pastor's car had a punctured tyre or developed a fault, pastor would send the key to his house, and he had to leave whatever he was doing to solve the problems with his own money and take the car to pastor's house. His family pushed pastor's car several times.

That happened literally every other day. Even late in the nights. To the extent, he was afraid to live on the same street with any pastor again.

Of course, it is not wrong to help your pastor if he has a challenge once in a while, I have enjoyed such assistance several times, but a situation where a pastor transfers his problem to another is bad, people should offer to help by themselves. And it ought not to be a daily occurrence.

Please try and understand. Leadership does not mean that people should be serving you.

3. Also Jesus took off his clothes so that we can know that it is not the cloth or vehicle we drive that makes us leaders.

Some years ago, around 1998 when this ministry began, I had two cars: a Benz and an old BMW. I employed a driver and a personal assistant who travelled with me everywhere. I was 'too big' to open the door by myself. I had a secretary who cleaned the office for me. I thought that was ministry. And God kept quiet.

Later I was invited to preach in a big church. Both of my vehicles were spoilt. But one was under repairs.

I prayed and pressured for it to be ready, but it was not. Therefore I did not honour the invite.

I wondered how a preacher of my status would arrive on Okada (commercial motorcycle) or in a taxi.

When God asked me questions about my failure to honour the invitation, I told him He was the one who failed me.

On a later date, I was angry with God because He did not provide me very good cars and He finally got across to me, that ministry is not measured by the kind of cloth I wear or the vehicle I drive. And He taught me to be simple in service and satisfied with whatever He provides for me.

For years after that I used the same vehicles. There was a time when the vehicles became so bad. I used triple adaptors on the engine of the Benz. I still have scars on one of my hands from reaffixing plugs that jumped out in motion. It smoked like a locomotive engine.

Of course, there were times and places where people looked down on me because of the vehicle I drove.

I remember a certain church where I was a guest. When I finished a powerful message everybody was jumping up in excitement. Then some of the leaders escorted me to the car. When the pastor saw my BMW he was so insulted that he had to pray for me there and then, requesting God to give me a replacement.

But since God explained to me earlier, it never mattered to me.

For the same reason, in later years, I could give out my only vehicle and go by public transport for 2 years.

I did that twice.

Today, I have vehicles, but I do not measure my status by the vehicle I drive.

We should be able to take off our dress (honour and glory) whenever necessary.

Prayer Points:

1. Jesus' knowledge of His position with God helped his humility. Open my understanding, so that I will know who I am.

2. Most times we are limited by others perception about us. We are always disturbed particularly when others look down at us. Deliver me from 'show ministry'.

Chapter Two

HE WASHED THE FEET OF HIS DISCIPLES

He was not complaining that they were dirty. Most people in leadership positions complain a lot. They often forget that they have the responsibility to take action.

As a leader, I have done this several times. I have complained to God several times about the church and what was happening there. But God would always remind me that I am the shepherd and a real shepherd would not complain about the sheep, he would herd them.

For instance, there was a time that no one gave in the church to support God's work. But as soon as I began to teach on that subject people began to respond.

The pastor is responsible either remotely or directly for everything seen in the church; just as a father is responsible for anything in his house.

He washed their feet. He did not plan to do it later. He did not procrastinate about it. Most leaders push the action till a later date, and they never really get round to do it.

Most of the great men in the Bible were prompt. For instance, each time God spoke to Abraham, he took a prompt action. It was the same with Moses.

In Acts 13:1-3 God instructed the Antioch church to release Paul and Barnabas to their ministry, and they acted immediately. Some others would still be holding vigils and praying some useless prayers when direction is clear.

A friend of mine worked with a ministry as a missionary. But at a point in time God began to ask him to leave the ministry, but because he loved the pastor and had a great reputation in that ministry, he did not pay attention to what God was saying, so he did not really understand the direction.

Unknown to him, that leader was already into immorality and several other errors and God was taking him out in view of dangers ahead.

Unfortunately therefore, my friend became afflicted.

Prompt actions must follow divine instructions. Otherwise, we could lose what God was trying to do with or for us. Such disobedience would also expose us to the devil's attack.

1. *Washing the feet of the disciples was an act of humility.*

When He did that, he was actually acknowledging that they were seemingly more important than he was. And that is true, the congregation or people are more important than the individual leader.

You exist for them.

Without the congregation your sermon is useless.

Without them, your grace cannot find expression.

Without the congregation, you don't have a ministry.

It is what you do to them, and through them that would fetch you a reward from God.

You need to humble yourself to serve them.

2. *Washing their feet was an act of love and assistance*

When Jesus did that, He went beyond his own interest and sacrificed His comfort to ensure that they were benefited.

Leadership involves a lot of sacrifices made for the followers, borne out of love and not as investments to yield a harvest later.

The Bible spoke about shepherds whose interest was milking the sheep for their own benefit. And in this action, He was telling us to do the opposite of that.

I remember a personal experience a few years ago. I took 2 ministers on my ministry assignment. When we finished, there was no money left to give them honoraria, because I had spent a lot of money to make the journey comfortable for them. However, since it was not my style to discuss the financial status, I just prayed and God told me to visit one of my partners who resided in one of the cities close by, on our way back.

Visiting him created a bit of inconveniences but the wilful offering he gave me was exactly what I needed to give them honoraria and enable them take gifts back home to their families.

What amazed me most in that journey was that both of them were angry with me: one, because that detour delayed the journey; and the other, because he thought I ought to give him more. Talk about perils of leadership!

3. *He did not wash their feet to derive a benefit. He just served them because they were children of God.*

When I served under leaders, I never expected any gift from any of my leaders at anytime.

I used to drive an elderly Methodist minister many years ago. I drove him from Ile-Ife to Okigwe, (Eastern Nigeria) Otukpo, (Middle belt of Nigeria) etc. He never needed to give me a gift. My joy was that I had the honour of serving God under him. He collected honoraria and never needed to share it with me.

Another leader I served under used to travel abroad regularly; it never occurred to me that he could bring anything for me. It never occurred to me that he could introduce me to travel abroad. Sincerely, I never expected any reward from him.

I travelled with him a few times, I never expected him to share his honoraria with me. And he never did. Why should he? When God eventually called me into vocational assignment, I struggled with Him, because I felt odd to be paid for my service unto God. I would prefer to serve without pay, but He explained to me that my work would be too difficult to combine with any other work, because I will travel a lot, I will have to prepare so many sermons, write so many books and spend so many hours in prayers as He would lead me.

And it has proven to be very true. The work I do is very enormous. But even now I still spend almost all the money I make, back on His work.

Leadership is not for benefit or reward.

When you see a church that is always improving their facilities, the pastor is responsible. When you see a church that is not improving their facilities, the pastor is equally responsible.

Development of facility takes a lot of sacrifice, both from the leader and his officers.

When you finally become a leader do not take any action to compel people to do things for you. For instance, don't tell them you are praying for them in a bid to receive gifts, it is a decent way of begging.

Jesus expects us to be his kind of leaders, who will serve the followers, not leaders who will use the followers for our own benefit.

Prayer Points:

1. Give me a heart to serve the people of God.
2. Show me the conflict between my desire and your desire for me. And give me the courage to submit to you.
3. Deliver me from crave for benefit or reward.

Chapter Three

LEADERSHIP IN THE KINGDOM

Then the mother of Zebedee's sons came to Him with her sons, kneeling down and asking something from Him. And He said to her, "What do you wish?" She said to Him, "Grant that these two sons of mine may sit, one on Your right hand and the other on the left, in Your kingdom." But Jesus answered and said, "You do not know what you ask. Are you able to drink the cup that I am about to drink, and be baptized with the baptism that I am baptized with?" They said to Him, "We are able." So He said to them, "You will indeed drink My cup, and be baptized with the baptism that I am baptized with; but to sit on My right hand and on My left is not Mine to give, but it is for those for whom it is prepared by My Father." And when the ten heard it, they were greatly displeased with the two brothers. But Jesus called them to Himself and said, "You know that the rulers of the Gentiles lord it over them, and those who are great exercise authority over them."Yet it shall not be so among you; but whoever desires to become great among you, let him be your servant. "And whoever desires to be first among you, let him be your slave-- "just as the Son of Man did not come to be served, but to serve, and to give His life a ransom for many."

Matthew 20:20-28

Only God knows how long this family had been planning and praying about their desire that was expressed here.

The two young men must have concluded that the best person to deliver the request was their mother. And they must have pleaded strongly with her on how to deliver the message. Finally, she summoned the courage, isolated the Lord and knelt before Him. They ensured that the others were not too close to argue, and placed their desire to the Lord.

In verse 24, the Bible indicated that the others were displeased with them because they made the request; certainly because they too wanted the same thing, and these guys were only faster. Is that not the way we all reason? 'Me, and me first!'

However, Jesus used that opportunity to explain a number of things to us about leadership in the Kingdom.

1. **It is foolish to seek position**, but better to seek to make huge sacrifices for the kingdom. Because when we get to heaven our reward would not be measured by position, but the amount of personal sacrifices we offered.

   In essence, in God's sight, the greater man is not the one with the biggest title or position, but the one who bears the worst pain for His sake. I guess that is why martyrs would receive a special honour.

   What pain have you endured for His sake?

   What rights, privileges, properties, comfort, etc, have you given up for Him?

   What or how much are you willing to give to Him with joy?

What makes us great leaders is not the title or position we occupy, but the amount of sacrifices we are making consistently for Him.

Several young people are eager today to receive calls, they are eager to follow the example of false prophets who live flamboyant and wasteful lifestyle; because they assume that it is a call to glory, wealth and blessing. They want to shine.

But divine call is either to die for Him or live for Him (meaning owning nothing, and accepting a frugal life of sacrifice with contentment, not minding what comes into your hands.)

Cease to pray for position, anointing, or ordination. Pray for grace to make more sacrifices for Him. Or better still; ask Him what more sacrifice He wants from you.

If you want to go into ministry to serve or to make more sacrifices, it is good. But my interest is that you need to understand that it is about sacrifice.

Serious, continuous, unending sacrifice!

That is the reason why a number of ministries don't pay their vocational ministers at all.

2. **Position is God's prerogative**. He lifts up one person and sets down another. You cannot decide what He would assign to you. His plan supersedes all.

   I was with an elderly man of God who was also a Medical Doctor some years ago. And he said, my brother I always envy you. I have been begging God for years, to allow me serve as a full-time (vocational) minister, but He did not allow me.

   And there are several others who were called to full time assignment and they attempted to run away.

   He is wise and sovereign.

3. **Position does not entitle you to lord it over your followers.** The word lord is actually an impossible word for a minister whose name actually means servant.

   How can a servant be lord at the same time? We are not meant to strike the brethren physically. We are not meant to use them to serve our own purposes, but to help them fulfil God's plan for them.

   They are not your servants, but your brethren. You are not meant to milk them, but to bless them.

You are not meant to compel them to do your will, but to coach them to recognize God's direction for them, and to do His will.

It is not wrong to be respected, honoured and celebrated, but it is wrong to allow men worship you. Let only God be Lord to them.

4. *Your main assignment is to be a servant, both to God and His children.*

A servant has no message of his own, but the Master's. A servant has no plan of his own, but the Master's. A servant does not dictate his assignment and destination, he just follows the Lord.

It is strange to say No Lord! But always Yes, Lord. The more God is using you to bless people in intercession, teaching, sharing, caring, support etc, the more a leader you are. You must get to know the people serving with you and the people you serve.

5. *You are not meant to be served like unbelievers.*

Leadership is not about people running errands for you. It is not about people giving and doing things for you, but you doing it for them. People may choose to help or bless you, but you don't demand for it.

You are not expected to be the first in line during distribution, but the last or the neglected.

People are not meant to be compelled to come and do your domestic chores for you.

You are not supposed to be like some evil prophets described in the Old Testament as shepherd who feed on the sheep and use them to fulfil their desires.

A fellow told me he wanted to be a minister. When I reminded him about the challenges, he told me his expected honoraria per month. Imagine, he had not even received a call yet, and he was calculating his income.

It should not be about self or benefit.

6. ***The way of God and His kingdom is humility.***

The lower you set yourself, the higher He rates you, and the higher, you set yourself, the less qualified you become for honour.

The higher you rise, the lower your voice should become in addressing people with dignity and respect.

The more God promotes you, the less you talk about yourself and your achievements. Beware of testimonies that tacitly promote you and your image.

The more you rise in position and status, the less you talk about it or even about yourself, e.g. your prayer life, miracles etc.

The more God uses you, the more you ensure that less of you is to be seen in it.

And that starts with the way you relate with your spouse. You must be quick to settle with your spouse. You must treat him/her with respect and prefer her.

7. **It is not your kingdom. It is not your property.** It is not your people. Everything belongs to God.

Often times, you see people who tell you; 'I have been serving everyone, now it is my time to go and do my own thing'. It is not your thing or church. Jesus is the owner of every vision.

Discipline too, is not about you, how you feel, what you think, but about Him and whatever He instructs.

It is not your glory. It is not your success

The failure cannot be yours, but His.

Prayer Points:

1. Deliver me from self.
2. This generation is crazy about titles and positions. Enable me to offer my body and self as a living sacrifice to you.
3. Help me to learn humility in my relationships, in my character, in ministry, in handling money and honour.
4. I know that those who fail to learn humility shall be humiliated. Please do not humiliate me.

Chapter Four

SERVANTHOOD IS THE LADDER

Jesus said

> *Anyone wanting to be a leader among you must be your servant. And if you want to be right at the top, you must serve like a slave. Your attitude must be like My own. For I did not come to be served, but to serve.*
>> Matthew 20:26 & 28 (Living Bible)

Then

> *But among you the one who serves best will be your leader.* Luke 22:26

These two verses are the foundation for Christian leadership.

What Jesus said here is the exact opposite of what the world says about who a real leader is.

In the world, you build a pyramid and you climb to the top, and stay at the top.

But Jesus said, "No, he who serves best leads best."

Servant-hood is leadership. The better you serve the more God raises you up to leadership.

Leadership is not a matter of getting people to serve your interests. Leadership is a matter of serving the best interests of others.

Jesus said, if you want to be great, you must learn to be the servant of all.

In essence stop looking for people or avenues through which people would serve you, but opportunities to serve believers.

What it means to serve others

Ordinarily, whatever service you render in church is service: ushering, singing in the choir, serving in technical units, teaching, preaching, membership of prayer squad, altar cleaning, general cleaning, decoration, chair arrangement, etc.

When you help someone in need anywhere, e.g., to carry a load, take a child or elderly across the road, care for the sick, help the disabled, help a pregnant lady with her load, help an accident victim, change a tyre, give money; when you go out of your way to assist your spouse, your parents, or anyone else in jobs not considered yours; when you go out of your way to hang out with some folks to encourage or bless them, certainly not for your own benefit; when you provide for a community, services that would benefit them, e.g. education (either as a proprietor or as a teacher), health, information, development, services like road repairs, weeding etc; praying for others; celebrating others, e.g. your parents, your spouse for her support and assistance, your boss, your workers, etc (certainly not yourself); giving what you have to another person: money, your seat in a crowded bus or bank, your comfort etc; and many more.

Chapter Five

SEVEN REASONS TO SERVE OTHERS

1. We were created to serve others

> *For we are His workmanship, created in Christ Jesus for good works, which God prepared beforehand that we should walk in them.* Ephesians 2:10

One reason why so many people are miserable today is because they have missed the purpose of life. They wait for people to serve them. Whereas, even before we were born, God planned a life of service for us.

As I serve others, my own needs are met and as I give my life away, I find it. You were created for service. If you are not serving somewhere, you are missing out on the very reason you were created.

As a leader, the more you serve with the right mind, the more fulfilling life becomes for you.

2. It proves that we belong to Christ.

God says that the way you know you are a part of the body of Christ is that you serve others. Serving is the proof of our identity as members of His family.

When you compel people to serve you and distance yourself from service, you are unlike Him. You could best be introduced as a bastard.

3. We serve God by serving others.

Serving others is the way to serve God.

> And whatever you do, do it heartily, as to the Lord and not to men, knowing that from the Lord you will receive the reward of the inheritance; for you serve the Lord Christ.   Colossians 3:23-24

No matter what you're doing, ensure, and remember that you're doing it for the Lord.

Don't ever imagine that the leader you are serving with is using you, or that the people are riding upon you. God enjoys the service of His saints.

> "And the King will answer and say to them, 'Assuredly, I say to you, inasmuch as you did it to one of the least of these My brethren, you did it to Me.'
> Matthew 25:40

4. We owe God everything.

> I beseech you therefore, brethren, by the mercies of God, that you present your bodies a living sacrifice, holy, acceptable to God, which is your reasonable service.
> Romans 12:1

He bought us at a very costly price. Therefore, He owns us.

The reason why we should make service our habit is what God has done for us, because of His mercy.

When I think of what Jesus Christ has done for me, the sacrifice that He has made for me, there is no sacrifice I can make for Him that will ever be too costly.

41

5. It's the best use of our lives and resources.

Therefore, my beloved brethren, be steadfast, immovable, always abounding in the work of the Lord, knowing that your labour is not in vain in the Lord.

1 Corinthians 15:58

How fulfilling it is to return home after a time of caring for the brethren, either in visitation or in hospital visit. Each time you give for a worthy course, you are full of joy.

Equally, when I go home and play with my kids; that is as important a service as preparing a sermon. When I take out the garbage or wash the dishes so that my wife or my kids can go do something else, that's just as significant service as when I am speaking to crowds of people because it all counts in God's eyes.

There is no job that can give your life a better value than serving others.

It is the best use of my life to serve other people. What counts for eternity is giving your life away in service, and not making money.

6. It makes life meaningful.

Jesus said

> *Only those who throw away their lives for My sake and the sake of the good news will ever know what it means to really live.*   Mark 8:35, (Living Bible)

It is silly to pity people who are serving God. If you're not serving, you're not living; you just exist.

It would preserve your life, and give you long life.

7. Serving will be rewarded for eternity.

Jesus said,

> *"If anyone serves Me, let him follow Me; and where 1 am, there My servant will be also. If anyone serves Me, him My Father will honour.*   John 12:26

He also says,

> *"His lord said to him, 'Well done, good and faithful servant; you were faithful over a few things, 1 will make you ruler over many things. Enter into the joy of your lord.'*   Matthew 25:21

There is a sure reward.

How you spend your time here is going to determine what would be done with you in the next life for eternity.

Whether you like it or not, you will stand before Jesus Christ after your sojourn on earth. I want to hear Him say to me, "Well done thou good and faithful servant. You were not perfect, but you did your best." That is why I must concentrate on my service.

At that point, when we meet Jesus, It will be worth it all.

Song:

1. Take my life, and let it be
   Consecrated, Lord, to Thee;
   Take my moments and my days,
   Let them flow in ceaseless praise.

2. Take my hands, and let them move
   At the impulse of Thy love;
   Take my feet and let them be
   Swift and beautiful for Thee.

3. Take my voice, and let me sing
   Always, only, for my King;
   Take my lips, and let them be
   Filled with messages from Thee.

4. Take my silver and my gold;

Not a mite would I withhold;
Take my intellect, and use
Every power as Thou shalt choose.

5. Take my will, and make it Thine;
It shall be no longer mine.
Take my heart; it is Thine own;
It shall be Thy royal throne.

6. Take my love; my Lord, I pour
At Thy feet its treasure-store.
Take myself, and I will be
Ever, only, all for Thee.

Prayer Points:
1. Lord I yield my life unto you for greater service of believers. From today I will serve more.

2. Help me to stop focusing on myself.

3. Create more opportunities for me to serve your children around me, and let me recognize the opportunities as they are created.

Other books by the same author

That Same Jesus
Joshua's Promotion
A New Life
The Lord is My Shepherd
Pursuit of Excellence
Procure Honour
The Power of Relationship
Aborted Priesthood
Essence of Marriage
Finding a Spouse
A New Beginning
Spiritual Contentions
God Answers Prayers
You Can Be Rich
Responsibilities in the family
Legacy of Service
Receiving Grace through the Anointing
Furrows of the Stream – a novel
Covenant of Son-ship

Arise and Shine
Making Right Choices
The Beauty of Obedience
The Honour of Representing God
The Sure Mercies of David
Walking with God
A Peculiar People
Running & Winning the Race
That Anger may send you to hell

www.ingramcontent.com/pod-product-compliance
Lightning Source LLC
Chambersburg PA
CBHW030306030426
42337CB00012B/605